AT HOME WITH
pattern

AT HOME WITH
pattern

SALLY CONRAN KATHERINE SORRELL

RYLAND
PETERS
& SMALL

LONDON NEW YORK

Designer Pamela Daniels
Senior editor Miriam Hyslop
Location research Tracy Ogino
Production Sheila Smith
Art director Anne-Marie Bulat
Publishing director Alison Starling

Styling Sally Conran
Text Katherine Sorrell

First published in the United States in 2006
by Ryland Peters & Small, Inc.
519 Broadway, 5th Floor
New York, NY 10012
www.rylandpeters.com

Printed in China

Library of Congress Cataloging-in-Publication Data
Sorrell, Katherine.
  At home with pattern / Katherine Sorrell, Sally Conran.
    p. cm.
  Includes index.
  ISBN-13: 978-1-84597-242-4
  ISBN-10: 1-84597-242-2
  1. Repetitive patterns (Decorative arts) in interior decoration.
  I. Conran, Sally. II. Title.
  NK2115.5.R45S67 2006
  747--dc22
                                    2006016110

contents

introduction

The Collins dictionary defines pattern as either "an arrangement of repeated or corresponding parts, decorative motifs, etc." or "a decorative design." But that does not necessarily help us to recognize the subtle differences between pattern and art, pattern and design, or simply pattern and a naturally occurring motif such as a row of seed heads or a flock of birds in the sky. Is a painting a pattern? How about a set of prints, each showing the same subject matter, reproduced in coordinating colors? Repetition, clearly, has something to do with it. But designs without repeats can also be patterns, and other factors, such as color, form, line, scale, and texture are also important. Perhaps the most helpful way to look at it is to say that, like music, poetry, dance, or even architecture, pattern is a way in which we strive to create order from the world around us, by using attractive repetition and/or variation. The eye attempts to find pattern in everything it sees; pattern surrounds us and can be found in all sorts of unexpected places.

Now is an exciting time for pattern, and particularly for using pattern in the home. Modern designers are using patterns with confidence, flair, and, sometimes, a tongue-in-cheek, self-aware sense of humor. Making the most of new techniques and materials, they are pushing the boundaries of pattern to the limits, developing innovative new styles and reinventing old ones, creating a look that is just right for right now.

Selecting patterns, not to mention combining them within a scheme, can be challenging, if not problematic, especially when we have become so accustomed to using plains. Interior design is an incredibly personal discipline, based entirely around your likes dislikes and how you want to live, and using pattern is just as personal. One person's ideal all-over print is another's cacophonous mess, so when it comes to using pattern in the home, it truly is up to you. Nevertheless, we have put this book together with the aim of helping you to make some of those decisions. We hope that it will inform and inspire you, offering insights into interesting, contemporary and, above all, beautiful and appealing ways in which pattern can be employed around the home, from the pretty to the sophisticated, the kitsch to the somewhat challenging.

We have divided modern pattern into five major themes, in order to narrow down the potentially mystifying diversity of patterns and to help you decide which types appeal to you and would work in your property. First, Nostalgia Revisited explores the use of the patterns of bygone eras—chintzes, tickings, and quirky 1950s prints, among others—in our homes. Opulent Glamour showcases glitzy, grown-up pattern. Characterized by sophisticated colors, textures, and bold lines, it is both luxurious and indulgent. Next, Bold and

Brave is a head-turning look. With its roots in 1960s style, it includes heavily stylized abstracts, geometrics, and florals, which are usually overscaled and drawn with bold lines or in flat blocks of unnatural color. Taking its lead from the natural world, Natural Inspirations offers an approach that is based on the timeless patterns that surround us, from a branch of blossoms to the grain of wood, updated for the modern home. Finally, Modern Classics are the enduring designs of the pattern world. Based on forms that evolved centuries ago, such as fleur de lys, medallions, urns, and Tudor roses, they use subtle colors and symmetrical, ordered patterns for a mature and serene effect.

Because pattern types are never clearly delineated, there is inevitably some overlap between themes, and some patterns do not fit neatly into any of the types. Within each chapter there is a broad spectrum of patterns, and these are shown put to use all around the house. Some of the ways in which pattern is applied are eminently practical; others are fairly eccentric. Wallpapers and fabrics (from curtains and upholstery to soft furnishings and accessories) dominate, because they are both the most widely available applications of pattern and also the easiest to use. Nevertheless, pattern is shown in other forms, too, from flatware and lampshades to floorings and cupboard doors; we have tried to demonstrate as wide a range as possible in order to enthuse and motivate you. We have explored just what comprises each type of pattern and why you might want to choose it, the types of home in which it might look its best and, probably most importantly, how to use it in order to make it work for you.

nostalgia revisited

There is something intrinsically appealing about the patterns of bygone eras. Whether a blowsy chintz, a mattress-ticking stripe, or even a quirky 1950s print, they stand for the opposite of today's fast-paced, mass-produced lifestyle, evoking a time when craftsmanship was, perhaps, a little more appreciated.

Nostalgic pattern celebrates the hand-made and the individual, produced with love and care—a pieced quilt, a hand-blocked wallpaper, a needlepoint cushion cover. Stitching, knitting, printing, lace-making, crochet, weaving, and other such time-consuming, traditional processes are the partners to this look, together with the use of charming, soft colors, often faded by time and wear.

Informal and easy-going, this is a look that is usually rather understated and, consequently, very comfortable to live with. It is not, however, necessarily an old-fashioned look. Although they can easily be used to create gently traditional interiors, the point about these nostalgic patterns is that they can also be reinterpreted in quite a modern way—by using fresh colorways, by juxtaposing them with pieces from other periods, or simply by paring everything down so that they become a focal point in a clean, minimal setting.

Nostalgic pattern evokes memories—real or imagined—of carefree living, of simple pleasures, and happy times. It is utterly appropriate as a quintessentially

ABOVE The woven geometric patterns of this pillow and throw are retro-inspired but modern in interpretation, in terms of both form and color. They work well with the mellow wood of the Victorian desk.

OPPOSITE A mix of pretty antiques and simple, modern furnishings provides the backdrop for the neutral tones of the traditionally-made Welsh textiles from Melin Tregwynt.

country or beach-house look, though would be just as much at home in a modern log cabin or a Scandinavian cottage, for example. It is pretty without being fussy, familiar without being predictable, and utilitarian without being dull. What it never is, though, is showy, loud, or hard-edged. The perfect complement to modest vernacular houses made from local materials, with log fires, small windows, and low ceilings, nostalgic pattern can also be used to lessen the imposing nature of a grander home, or to soften a modern property, adding interest and personality to what may be otherwise bland or harsh features.

Broadly speaking, there are three main types of nostalgic pattern: geometrics, florals, and retro.

THIS PAGE A wooden floor, tongue-and-groove walls, upholstered armchair, and wool blanket—this cozy corner is highly nostalgic, but has been given a modern edge by the graphic quality and slightly acidic tones of the blanket's dots.

The geometrics consist of spots, stripes, checks, and other basic patterns produced from circles, squares, diamonds, rectangles, and so on. In fabrics, they may be printed but are often woven—a natural result of the manufacturing process. Mattress ticking, a heavy cotton woven in one-color stripes on a cream or white background, is a good example, being functional and versatile; polka dots (often white on a one-color background) and gingham, a small checked, two-color cotton weave, are others. A block-printed wallpaper with wide stripes is suitably pretty but plain, as are tiled floors laid in a checkerboard pattern, ceramics decorated with stripes or dots, and rugs woven in simple patterns. Colors are generally in the pastel or neutral/natural range, though the occasional primary makes its presence known. In the pattern spectrum these are among the most low-key, and they are an ideal choice for anyone who is nervous about using pattern in their home. They work well with solids, but are also easy to combine with the next grouping of nostalgic pattern: florals.

There is a wealth of floral patterns to choose from, with something to suit everyone's taste. The ones that are most appropriate for the modern nostalgic look are those that could loosely be described as "pretty" rather than formal or striking. An ideal choice is chintz, officially a polished cotton printed in several colors on a white or pale background, though these days the term has come to

TOP LEFT **The rounded squares of these patterned cushions are reminiscent of the 1950s.**

TOP RIGHT **A large paisley print in a neutral color is the focal point in a gently classic room.**

ABOVE **An antique French chandelier is an ideal accessory for the nostalgic look.**

ABOVE When combining two or more patterns, it is important to match colors exactly. These two patterns are wildly different, but the coordination of the blue and yellow/gold means that they can sit next to each other quite comfortably.

RIGHT This sofa, a thrift-shop find, was given a slipcover with a country-style ruffle. The fabric, with a 1950s-style monkey pattern, was picked up for peanuts in a market. The flowery curtains are a bold stroke—they do not match the sofa exactly, but the colors are right and, given the eclectic nature of the room as a whole, it all somehow seems to work.

mean almost any multicolored floral fabric or transfer-printed china. Most people think of chintz as a peculiarly English phenomenon, but it actually originated in India, a hand-blocked fabric made using brightly colored dyes from local plants and featuring fashionable Indian designs. Chintz was first imported to England in the 17th century, and soon became enormously fashionable. English designers sent patterns over to the Indian printers and dyers, and the fabrics gradually began to incorporate English plants and designs. In the 19th century, Lancashire mills mechanized the printing process, making English chintz available to people from all walks of life. Chintz earthenware also became hugely popular—in the 19th century, the Staffordshire potteries were able to make transfer-printed chintz earthenware (with all-over patterns that emulated the fabrics) that was cheap enough for everyday use; gradually it crossed the Atlantic, with the early 20th century seeing a chintz-collecting craze in North America that has never quite subsided.

A natural, flowing style of chintz is perfect for this look, and it follows that the ideal plants depicted are those cottage-garden species such as roses, hollyhocks, foxgloves, lupines, peonies, hydrangeas, poppies, bluebells, and the like. In addition to chintz, floral patterns reproduced or derived from 18th- or 19th-century historical documents are a good choice, too, especially the ones that are relatively small in scale or that use soft color combinations on a pale background. And, of course, there are plenty of modern designers who produce

ABOVE **Nothing could be more nostalgic than a tapestry cushion with patterns of both flowers and the Union Flag.**

OPPOSITE **In this cozy room, pieces and patterns from different periods add up to an appealing whole. Chesterfield sofas are covered in plain, striped, and floral fabrics; the blind is a 19th-century English print by Bennison, and the wall hanging a patchwork that took the owner five years to make.**

THIS PAGE AND OPPOSITE, BELOW RIGHT Tapestries, rugs, and paintings in jewellike colors are the focal point in this house, offset by soft pink walls and curtains and golden floorboards.

OPPOSITE, LEFT AND ABOVE RIGHT This pink satin pillow has an extravagant ruffle that would suit an Edwardian undergarment. It adds a sassy feel to the classically patterned sofa upholstery and the sweet retro fabric on the wall.

desirable floral patterns which, while having a nostalgic feel, are also fresh and updated for a contemporary home.

As for using florals, curtains, upholstery, and wallpapers are the obvious choices, with the addition of cushions, throws, and wall hangings. Floral rugs and even carpets are becoming increasingly fashionable once again, while chintz- and other floral-printed or painted ceramics are utterly gorgeous. Hand-painted floral tiles could look charming as a kitchen or bathroom backsplash, and accessories might take the form of oven gloves, tea cozies, or even dish towels.

The third category, retro, is very different. This features mid-20th-century prints with their characteristic molecular, kitsch, and primitive designs, sometimes featuring black, gray, and white, but often

in clashing colors such as mustard, lime, and tomato red. Boomerang, kidney, hourglass, and palette shapes are absolutely typical of these patterns, as are molecular shapes, a result of an initiative by the 1951 Festival of Britain to bring decoration up to date by harnessing the scientific advances of the time as a basis for new designs. Using blueprints of crystal structures, designers produced abstract patterns that proved most desirable. Also popular were motifs inspired by primitive or surreal art, such as the paintings of Paul Klee or Joan Miró, and images from popular culture such as cartoons or cowboys or food and drink. Such patterns tend to be rather flat and stylized, sometimes with flowing, illustrative lines, but they are always highly recognizable. Enduring motifs such as the Union Flag or Stars and Stripes are also characteristic of this look, as are modern, 1950s-inspired designs of poodles, sailing yachts, cabbage roses, and the like.

OPPOSITE **A mix of inviting seating, upholstered in warm colors and soft textures, is made all the more appealing by an eclectic use of pattern, in the form of chintz, two-tone florals, and a mid-sized check.**

LEFT **A rather serious stripe and a variety of florals have been layered together here. It works because not all of the patterns are very dense, and the colors have been matched almost exactly.**

LEFT AND ABOVE The tongue-in-cheek Union Flag wall hanging is the focal point in this room. It sets the scene for a modern-retro vibe, and other furnishings have, wisely, been kept to a minimum. Walls, floor, and upholstery are as plain as could be, but the striped blinds and floral cushions (densely patterned, but on a white background) make for a relaxed feel.

Retro patterns can be used very effectively in kitchens and eating areas, where they make lovely highlights, perfect for dishes and food storage containers, table linen, dining chair cushions, and pictures hung on the walls. Geometrics are another option for these rooms, and checked tablecloths (perhaps oilcloth), striped seat covers, and spotted coffee mugs all spring to mind. Both look great when used in combination with retro-style appliances (or, at least, nothing too sleek and 21st-century) and such accessories as enamel jugs, wicker baskets, colored toasters, and chrome kettles.

Florals really come into their own in the bedroom, where they are ideally suited to creating an intimate, personal, warm, and cozy space which might be too much elsewhere. Layer upon layer can, if you wish, be used here, in the form of eiderdowns, quilts and bedcovers, curtains and blinds, covered headboards, carpets or rugs, cushions and chair covers, lampshades and, of course, wallpapers.

In the living room, meanwhile, nostalgic patterns of any type will make an impact, whether as dashes of interest in an otherwise subdued room or combined to form a more complete and overall look. They can be

employed as fabric on sofas and chairs, for cushions and

throws, pictures or framed prints, curtains, wall hangings,

lampshades, and rugs. Overall, these patterns are best

teamed with old and beautifully worn, warm woods—oak and

pine, say, rather than pale beech or ash, or dark mahogany—

and other natural materials such as leather, wicker, wool, and

stone. Bare floorboards, milk paints, shuttered windows,

stoves, iron radiators, and other traditional but low-key

ABOVE These geometric cushion covers are Moroccan; the floral one is made from a vintage silk scarf. Not everyone could mix these dense patterns and vivid colors, but the owner of this house has a fantastic eye and is not afraid to experiment.

features form their natural backdrop—
definitely nothing too modern, machine-
made, sleek, or perfect.

Even the pattern novice will find that it is
not difficult to use nostalgic patterns
successfully. The obvious starting point is to
decide where you stand in the pattern
stakes—retro, geometric, or floral—and how
far you want to go with the look. Adding a
dash of interest with the occasional cushion,
tile or papered wall is one thing, but creating
an entirely patterned environment is quite
another. If you prefer a pared-down look,
restrict yourself to just a few accessories;
otherwise, feel free to pile pattern upon
pattern, perhaps stripes and checks with
florals of different types. This layered effect
looks amazing when done well, and is not so

OPPOSITE **In this timeless, calm, table setting, the shapes of these elegant ceramics are traditional, but their patterns—large dots in subtle colors—are anything but.**

LEFT AND ABOVE **A blue and white checked tablecloth with striped and floral cushion covers and a Union Flag doormat—an ideal combination for a nostalgic dining room. A predominant use of white gives the room a clean, modern feel.**

LEFT AND OPPOSITE These Delft-style tiles were hand-painted specifically for the kitchen and breakfast room of this house by the owner. He tracked down vignettes in old cook books, painted them onto white tiles, and had them fired in Scotland. They work perfectly with a floral tablecloth and Middle Eastern rug, and as a backdrop to the cream Aga range.

ABOVE The varying patterns of these kitchen accessories are pulled together by their pretty cobalt blue.

hard to achieve as it might seem. Of course, much of it is down to surety of eye and innate good taste, but there are some basic guidelines which will help.

First, color. Nostalgic patterns can come in a wide range of colors, but there are limits to how many can be combined in one space, and even the most eclectic room should have some sense of order to look attractive. It makes sense, when combining patterns, to choose designs that have one or more colors in common, ensuring visual coherence. So the background of a floral might, for example, coordinate with one of the colors in a check. Unfortunately,

though, it isn't always that simple, because the dominant colors of a multicolored pattern aren't always the ones that cover the largest area. To make sure that you know what colors will be most visible in each pattern that you choose, it is advisable to stand well back and assess them carefully: warm colors, such as vivid red, will leap forward, while cool colors, such as blue and green, will tend to recede. It is also a good idea to choose, as a basis for the scheme, a selection of colors from the same "family"—which could mean either blues, pinks, yellows, and so on, or pastels, secondaries, neutrals, and the like.

The exception here is bold, primary colors—most rooms (and people) can't take a grouping of lots of really strong colors together. Then, when your main selection is done, work in highlights of contrasting colors to make the result more interesting. And, because dense patterns can tend to fight with one another, it is wise to put a busy pattern against another that is much simpler.

Having worked out a comfortable balance of colors, consider the scale of each pattern. Patterns that are all of the same or similar scale might appear boring, but mixing very large with very small prints is not always a good idea—the eye can find the jump disturbing. When mixing floral patterns, for example, you could compare it to designing a garden border. You would not plant hydrangeas,

OPPOSITE AND LEFT **An unconventional use of pattern is the hallmark of this house, and here a 1950s fabric print by Florence Broadhurst has been placed on 1970s plastic dining chairs, while the floor is made from Dutch café tiles dating from the early 20th century and the 1950s.**

ABOVE **The focal point of this dining area is a framed chintz—in fact, a thrift shop sample, in an old, repainted frame. Vivid flower patterns are teamed with stripes and patchwork, and a mix of furniture from around the world.**

with their large, round heads of flowers, next to tiny forget-me-nots; it would be incongruous. Instead, just as in the garden, use small with medium patterns, or medium with large, contrasting the shapes (long and thin, circular, curving) for variety. Do not forget that small-scale patterns, especially in pale colors, are only really noticeable close up; from a distance they look like a plain color. This may be an advantage, as you could use a spriggy floral or tiny checked wallpaper, for example, and it would be a subtle addition to a scheme that calls for a decorative element while retaining a sense of airy spaciousness.

Experiment until you reach an overall effect with which you are happy. A good starting point is to stick to white or pale backgrounds and two or three small- and medium-scale patterns that have a key color in common. If in doubt, choose a piece that you adore—a lovely old tile, an eiderdown, or a jug, for example— and repeat its style or color of pattern in other pieces. Then vary the theme by choosing a pattern in similar style but complementary colors, and perhaps a slightly different scale, and continue in this vein.

Where to look for nostalgic patterns? The easiest place to start is to scour the high street. For an element of luxury, you could incorporate more expensive, high-end, or limited-edition designs. Using only new elements, however, will not strike the authentic note of true nostalgia, which consists of a mix of cherished old possessions, family heirlooms, attractive hand-me-downs, second-hand discoveries, saleroom bargains, the odd classic antique, and just

OPPOSITE **These little bags provide a point of interest in an otherwise minimal bedroom. They are made from scraps of Bennison fabric, the patterns reproduced from 17th- and 18th-century designs to look old and faded.**

ABOVE **Framed fabric has been used to add decorative interest to the walls of this bedroom. Its white background is echoed by the white-painted frame and the bedcover.**

one or two newer pieces. If you aren't lucky enough to have been given the perfect Welsh blanket or 1950s coffee pot from granny's attic, then patience, perseverance, and a nose for a good find enter the picture. Much of the enjoyment of creating this look is in the seeking out of amazing pieces, forgotten treasures, beautiful remnants, and incredible bargains. Sifting through thrift stores and yard sales will probably yield the cheapest finds. Then there are auctions and antiques shops, where you may pick up fabric, china, rugs, art, and other pieces at a snip, or pay enormous amounts for items of known provenance

and genuine quality. You can also make things yourself: piecing together remnants into a quilt, framing a scrap of old wallpaper as an eye-catching print, or turning a monogrammed linen sheet into a curtain. Make do and mend, recycling, and reusing are at the heart of this look, and in many cases the more worn and faded a piece of fabric, the better. A few chips on a jug, a threadbare area on a rug—minor imperfections may well be an enhancement rather than a problem. The heart and soul of nostalgic pattern, after all, is in a judicious but artless mix of things from a variety of sources, resulting in a look and feel that is uniquely personal.

THIS PAGE A simple but effective combination of two differently scaled florals and a check in a co-ordinating color. The predominance of white as a background makes the look fresh and clean.

OPPOSITE, LEFT AND RIGHT Romantic and pretty, this modern Cath Kidston print wallpaper is based on a retro design. Used in this small room with a sloping ceiling, it is deliberately all-enveloping, with a charming, sophisticated-country feel.

LEFT AND ABOVE In this large conservatory, the densely patterned Berber pillows provide splashes of color around a plain wooden dining table. Generous arrangements of flowers in assorted receptacles (including a coffee pot) echo their shades. The white-painted brick wall is covered in a variety of watercolor prints, of Moroccan souks and the Italian lakes. They were all found in thrift stores and happened to be in coordinating black frames. It is an eclectic collection, but somehow it all works marvelously.

SUCCESS WITH NOSTALGIC PATTERN

Nostalgic patterns celebrate the handmade and individual, and look wonderful when combined with pieces made by traditional processes: tapestry, lace, block-printed fabrics or wallpapers, patchwork, knitting, handmade ceramics, and hand-painting are all good choices.

Geometrics work well as a foil for florals or for retro patterns; it is trickier to make other combinations work, but with careful consideration of color, scale, and density, unusual mixtures can look wonderful.

Nostalgic patterns can look traditional (though never grand or imposing) or timeless, or may have a fresh, modern edge. Color, scale, and how densely they are layered all determine their effect. Large-scale patterns in neutral colors or on white backgrounds have a more contemporary feel, while smaller, busier patterns used more extensively, or in conjunction with other nostalgic patterns, have a more old-fashioned look.

The three main types of nostalgic pattern are florals, geometrics, and retro. Look for chintzes and other florals either derived from historical documents or in relatively small scale and pretty colors; basic patterns of dots, stripes, and checks, or variations of these; and mid-century prints or ones with an element of kitsch.

Colors are often soft and understated, in the pastel range and perhaps deliberately faded, though brighter and neutral shades play a part, too.

A good starting point when using nostalgic pattern is to take a piece that you really love, whether it is a handmade pot, a patchwork quilt, or a painted tile, and echo either its color or pattern style in other areas. The fun is in the finding of great things from all sorts of sources, whether the mall, auction, thrift shop, or hardware store. Try not to be too formal—the essence of this look is easy-going, mix and match, and intrinsically personal to you.

opulent glamour

OPPOSITE AND BELOW
There's no mistaking the wow-factor in this loft apartment. Combined with sleek, sometimes oversized furnishings, the patterns are monochrome, large-scale, non-naturalistic, and open in design. They are used as dramatic points of emphasis in a space that is otherwise pared down in color, though luxurious in texture and metallic shimmer.

RIGHT This side table was custom-made by printing a glamorous wallpaper onto acrylic.

Glamorous patterns are glitzy, grown-up, and luxurious. They are superbly dramatic and capable of bringing wow-factor to any home.

Characterized by monochrome colors and bold lines, opulent, glamorous patterns are not defined by any particular design styles. Florals, geometrics, abstracts, or figurative patterns may all be involved—it has more to do with color, texture, scale, and how they are used than what they actually consist of.

The color range for this style is strictly sophisticated. Primaries are generally too harsh, pastels too soft; instead, black, ivory, gray, turquoise, crimson, eggplant, taupe, and chocolate take center stage, alongside gold, silver, pewter, bronze, and other metallics or pearlescents. A subtle, or even not-so-subtle shimmer, shine, or luster is highly desirable. As important as color is texture. The lush pile of velvet, the soft density of flock, the high gloss of glazed ceramic, or the sheen of satin all have the luxurious feel that is essential here.

Just as colors are heightened and textures conspicuous, the scale of glamorous patterns is larger than life. Forget petite repeats, daintiness, or subtle intricacy—this is all-out, look-at-me, bold scale.

OPPOSITE **The striking rose pattern is, in fact, a "paint-it-yourself" canvas.**

LEFT **Graphic floral crockery (by Jasper Conran for Wedgwood) echoes the rose painting and contrasts wonderfully with the 1960s black fiberglass table.**

ABOVE **An elongated and embossed coffee pot, based on a design from the 1960s, adds a decorative, rococo touch, while the gold candelabrum with a cherub base is pure, opulent glamour.**

The patterns themselves tend to be open rather than dense, however, with a relatively pale background, which provides a visual "breather" and means that they are striking rather than overwhelming. Style-wise, flowers, leaves, and plants feature heavily, but do not include naturalist reproductions. As well as their scale being altered for dramatic effect, outlines are simplified, more so than with other types of pattern, so that colors can be limited and used in large blocks. Florals frequently tend toward an abstract or geometric look; geometrics, meanwhile, often have an opulent, Art Deco-inspired appearance.

Although this look is utterly up to the minute, the provenance of the patterns themselves is immaterial. A wallpaper or fabric could just as easily feature a pattern from the 17th or 19th centuries as the 21st,

THIS PAGE The funky 1960s furnishings in this home are complemented by flea-market finds and a pair of pillows made from vintage silk scarves, by Maisonette.

OPPOSITE This hotel suite in Amsterdam houses a confident mix of avant-garde furnishings by leading international designers. The stunning wall panel by Bisazza is a tiled mosaic, its pattern computer-generated in a range of monochrome shades. The "crochet" table by Moooi adds another subtle layer of pattern.

provided it displays the right characteristics of color, scale, density, and stylization. What makes the look so up to date is the style of approach, the confidence of use, and the slick presentation of carefully combined elements. Similarly, the processes used to manufacture the patterned wallpaper, fabrics, furniture, flooring, and accessories involved could be deeply traditional. Items made by hand-printing, knotting, stitching, or glazing may sit side by side with pieces created using 21st- century technologies such as digital printing, computer manipulation, or laser-cutting, for example. Whatever the techniques involved, however, this is not a look that cuts corners or uses cheap materials. It is about polished perfection—whether made by man or machine—and nothing less.

Glamorous, opulent patterns work particularly well in large spaces—lofts and converted industrial buildings, for example, or generously proportioned period homes.

LEFT AND OPPOSITE **Using just one large work of art (here, another "paint-it-yourself" canvas) is a great way to add drama to a room. This piece is quite bold in style but, teamed with smoky gray and pink glass, metal, and rosewood, the overall effect is glamorous. The lampshade is lined with fabric by Marimekko— note how the limited range of colors in this room gives it a sophisticated appearance.**

Here they come into their own as a style for someone who is not afraid to make a statement. That said, when used judiciously they can be just the thing for livening up a small, boring space, providing an atmosphere of intimate luxury, even decadence. These patterns look expensive, though they do not necessarily have to cost a fortune. Yes, it is easily possible to spend big bucks on high-quality materials and finishes, designer one-offs, and unique installations. But with ingenuity it is just as possible either to make inexpensive finds appear much more costly or to use pricey pieces in limited quantities so that they give the desired overall effect.

These patterns also look sleek, sophisticated, and internationally appealing; vernacular culture is given a miss in favor of globe-crossing worldliness, so what looks great in a New York high-rise appears just as

OPPOSITE **In another context this wallpaper might look rather traditional, but its deep, sophisticated color brings it bang up to date, especially when teamed with slimline, overscaled modern furniture.**

THIS PAGE **A carved and painted French bed sets the tone for this opulent bedroom, its walls covered in a relief paper by Anaglypta, which creates a barely-there pattern in itself. The pillow covers are, again, made from vintage silk scarves, and the 1960s Italian light was found in a market.**

good in a Stockholm townhouse. The spirit of the city is inherent in this look. It's sexy, sassy, and mature, appealing to the well-traveled type who is accustomed to airport lounges, valet parking, and room service.

Practicalities tend not to be the foremost consideration when working with glamorous patterns, yet it is perfectly possible to create rooms in this style that are both functional and sensational to look at. While essentially decorative, glamorous pattern can be used for almost any application that you can think

of, from walls and floors to furnishings and accessories.

When planning an overall scheme, it is the rooms and spaces that are most public, such as hallways and living rooms, that can be the ultimate showstoppers, full of glamorous pattern in the form of papered walls, curtains, upholstery, lampshades, and rugs. The same goes for dining areas, where lavish entertaining and lavish pattern can go hand in hand—the latter could be in the form of wall, floor, or furniture coverings, or accessories such as china and glassware. Bedrooms, being more private, suit a sensual approach, perhaps using just one pattern for walls, curtains, or bed linen, or choosing subdued colors and emphasizing texture instead. Kitchens are more difficult, as they are dominated by storage cupboards, which tend to be relatively plain. There is no reason,

LEFT Wallpaper with a metallic sheen is perfect for a dreamy, feminine bedroom. This "Cranes" pattern, custom-printed in white and silver, is by renowned wallpaper designer Florence Broadhurst, whose work from the 1960s and 1970s is enormously fashionable again today.

OPPOSITE This charming, quirky chandelier is actually made from two lights wired together.

however, why elements of the room could not be given the glamorous treatment: a backsplash, for example, could be tiled with mosaic in a sumptuous pattern or a floor could be covered with a custommade design in vinyl. And bathrooms are the new living rooms, palaces of indulgence filled with the utmost in luxury, and it follows that opulent pattern will look fabulous here, usually in the form of tile work, but possibly also damp-resistant wallpaper, flooring, or an item of furniture such as a stool, chair, or screen.

To use opulent, glamorous pattern successfully requires vision and a strong sense of style. A half-hearted approach is likely to be a disaster, as this look requires a good overview of the end result; it is probably best approached when redecorating an entire room rather than as a piecemeal project. Although this is far from being a minimal look, furnishings should, on the whole, be sleek and

OPPOSITE **This dramatic wallpaper in two-tone blue and gold is by Florence Broadhurst, whose trailblazing designs combine exquisite hand-printing with vibrant colors and confident, dynamic forms. Called "Spotted Floral," its twisting outlines echo those of the eccentric wall light.**

ABOVE LEFT AND ABOVE **The patterns and colors of this tiled floor combine wonderfully as a backdrop to the blues and golds of the wall and screen. The floor was reclaimed from a Dutch house and each individual tile had to be cleaned carefully by hand before it could be relaid.**

BELOW **1930s-style geometric wallpaper panels have been used to add glamorous, graphic pattern. Their reflective quality gives the space a light and airy atmosphere. Overhead, a 1960s pendant light adds yet more individuality, while on the stairway it is just possible to see the corner of a modern portrait made from multicolored sequins.**

OPPOSITE **In this imposing hallway, the twining pattern of the wallpaper is traditional, but its gold shimmer is anything but, while the enormous chandelier is another classic piece that has been updated, with vibrant pink shades. A plain floor and white woodwork mean that the overall look isn't overwhelming.**

chic. While there is no need for a room to seem bare, it is better that it is a little pared down than crowded with unnecessary items of furniture. When in doubt, opt for less rather than more, and plain furnishings rather than ornamental. That way, you can leave the pattern to do the talking.

Contrasts of style can be an important factor in creating this look, so period details such as crown molding cornices, high baseboards, or elaborate fireplaces can appear fantastic teamed with modern patterns while, conversely, traditional patterns are amazing in combination with ultra-modern furnishings. The place to start is with the architecture of your home, and the furnishings that you own already. Mixing old and new is great, but does require that you limit the mixture to details and pieces that really work together; that have some kind of similarity of scale, of outline, of color or texture, of material or aesthetic influence. When you know where you stand in this respect, it is possible to give consideration to the patterns and colors that will complement your existing possessions.

The next step is to select a limited palette of colors and patterns; you can always add more later. As mentioned previously,

monochromes make the kind of strong statement that best suits this look anyway, while combining more than a couple of these types of eye-catching patterns might be overpowering. Then, decide where these patterns are best applied. For this style, the obvious, and most straightforward, applications are in the form of one wall covered in a dramatic paper or a sofa or chair upholstered in an opulent fabric. In a kitchen or bathroom, an area of mosaic tiling is relatively simple, and not necessarily terribly expensive, to achieve. Less permanently, adding patterned pillows, lampshades, bedcovers, throws, table linen, or rugs, and small display accessories such as vases, plates, or pots, is an inexpensive and easy way to create this look. Clever tricks might include framing a piece of metallic wallpaper and hanging it like a work of art, or collecting small lengths of expensive fabric and using them as a simple blind or a wide border on the bottom of a curtain. Taking it a stage further, a room with all four walls covered in glamorous wallpaper can look amazing (best kept to large spaces, however), as can an entire set of furniture upholstered in complementary patterned fabrics, and you may wish to consider installing multicolored floorings such as tiles, vinyl, or carpet. For greater complexity, the ultimate achievement is to layer glamorous pattern upon pattern—curtains with upholstery with cushions with wallpaper, perhaps. Choose with confidence and the results will be stunning.

OPPOSITE AND ABOVE **Wall-to-wall mosaic tiling by Bisazza proves that large-scale pattern can look fantastic in a bathroom.**

TOP LEFT AND RIGHT **It is possible to use wallpaper in a bathroom that does not get too moist and steamy. Here, an acrylic backsplash protects the glamorous paper without hiding it.**

SUCCESS WITH GLAMOROUS PATTERN

This is a sophisticated and mature look that says showstopping, city-style, look-at me luxury. It works best in large spaces and when combined with modern or mid-20th-century furniture; polished perfection is the overall aim.

Sophisticated colors characterize these patterns, along with large-scale, open designs that are strong and non-naturalistic. Texture is as important as color—think silk, velvet, and satin, flock, highly glazed ceramic, polished wood, leather, and suede. Lustrous, metallic, and pearlescent sheens are also highly desirable.

Look for stylized floral patterns with bold outlines on an open background, and geometrics with an Art Deco-influenced appearance. 1960s prints and computer-generated modern designs also play a part in this look. Traditional patterns can work well when translated into modern colors and textures.

Concentrate on a limited use of color, with varied textures and chic, mostly clean-lined, perhaps overscaled furniture. Confidence in approach is key, and it is advisable to plan an entire room in one go.

Contrast modern furnishings with period architectural details, antiques, and bargain finds for interest. The patterns themselves may be traditional or modern—what matters is their color, scale, and texture, and the way in which they are used.

A great way to introduce this look to almost any home is by covering one wall in a textured or metallic wallpaper, hanging a large-scale print or framed length of fabric, tiling a backsplash, or adding one or two smaller pieces such as a rug, bedcover, lampshade, or some cushions. If in doubt, opt for less rather than more. You can always add later.

BELOW AND OPPOSITE
Hexagonal wallpaper by Marcel Wanders covers one wall of an ultra-modern Amsterdam hotel room. Its unusual style sets the tone for the entire space, in which a lean, boxy sofa is covered in a graphic, abstract print that employs strong colors and unusual forms, and an enormous lamp oversees everything.

Bold and brave is a head-turning look: it is pattern out to make a statement. Dynamic, hard-hitting, and generally quite masculine, it might sometimes even be called loud. Abstracts, geometrics, and florals are heavily stylized, usually overscaled, and drawn with bold lines or in flat blocks of unnatural color.

Delicacy is not the issue here; it is impact that matters. The roots of this look are in 1960s style—the era of youth and rebellion, when fashionable culture revelled in the ephemeral, the innovative, and the zany. Motifs came from film, music, television, comics, adverts, and everyday items such as seaside postcards or domestic appliances, using vibrant, self-assured colors such as orange, yellow, purple, green, crimson, and silver. Abstract geometric shapes and dots were also popular, as were the swirling geometric shapes of Op Art, often in monochromes, especially black and white. Later in the same decade, and into the 1970s, patterns were strongly influenced by psychedelia, which arose largely from the Californian hippy movement. Influenced by Art Nouveau, free love, Eastern religions, and drug culture, it featured amoeba-like patterns and clashing, acid colors.

Contemporary bold pattern takes elements of the above and updates them for the 21st century. Well-defined outlines and dense

patterning in abstract forms are key. Rather than a plain, pale background that provides a relief for the lines and shapes of the pattern itself, in this case there is no distinction and the entire field comprises an all-over pattern. As for colors, you can't go wrong if you emulate the striking combinations of Italian fashion labels Emilio Pucci and Missoni (both of which were big influences on the 1960s fashion scene), in which a number of different shades are combined, sometimes graduating, sometimes involving apparently

ABOVE AND OPPOSITE Bold patterns can be very straightforward to use, creating an instant effect. Here, the owner of this light-filled city apartment has chosen a selection of pillows by fashionable New York designer Jonathan Adler. Their 1960s-inspired patterns are a variation on a geometric theme, and they employ vivid, coordinating colors to make a great focal point in an otherwise relatively plain room.

clashing colors for overall effect.

Scale and color are important features of bold pattern, and most bold patterns are reasonably large in scale or strong in color; generally both. However, all genres of pattern consist of a spectrum, a range of patterns that fit within the category but that vary in degree, some of them falling slap bang in the middle of the definition, others at one end or other. As a group, they hang together, but they are by no means identical—which is what makes pattern so infinitely enjoyable, both to use and

LEFT In this masculine apartment, pattern has been used with careful consideration and combined with sophisticated modern furnishings. The backdrop is a floor in polished American walnut, and in the dining area the table is spray-coated aluminum, with leather chairs all around. The patterned pillows and upright chair are in an Osborne & Little fabric that combines orange, green, and chocolate in a modern-retro weave. They stand out because all the other furnishings in the room are plain—though the upholstery on the chairs includes heathery colors that are picked up in the stronger patterns.

BELOW The rug is in a larger version of the pillow pattern, and was, in fact, the starting point for the overall design of the room.

to live with. So, when using bold pattern in real life, there are occasions when a smaller scale pattern can be used in vivid colors, or when pale or soft colors are used for a large-scale pattern, and the overall effect, though not absolutely characteristic of its genre, can still be termed bold. For those who are wary of surrounding themselves with look-at-me pattern, yet still enjoy its character, this is a good route to take.

If you are considering whether or not to use bold pattern in your home, the answer probably lies in your own personality. Because, unless you decide to apply

bold designs only to very limited areas, you are committing yourself to a scheme that is audacious and all-encompassing. If you have the flair and confidence to do it well, it can look amazing. So, ask yourself whether you feel absolutely comfortable in a dramatic, rich environment, and whether vibrant colors really are your thing.

While bold patterns can certainly look wonderful in period properties, especially those of a grand nature, they really suit the neat, rectilinear shapes of modern homes—the more minimal the better, with clean lines,

THIS PAGE AND OPPOSITE
The dramatic stripes are an
Osborne & Little wallpaper. Silver
is used to unify the apartment
throughout, and the broad stripes
lead the eye from the front door
to the terrace, where there is a
fabulous view of the River Thames.

high ceilings, large windows, and plain surfaces. Their natural partners are modern materials such as plastic, resin, stainless steel, and glass, and furniture that is sleek, slim, and unfussy. For a really chic, fashionable look they can be used in a postmodern way, where the usual forms of different materials are subverted or the conventional proportions of furnishings are altered.

These patterns also look amazing in retro-style homes, where they can be teamed with furnishings that either date from or are reminiscent of 1960s and 1970s, involving curving, molded shapes, or low, lean lines. Think lava lamps, spherical televisions, hippy-style rattan pieces, and stacking chairs by Robin Day and Verner Panton. These patterns are, however, best avoided in low-ceilinged, wood-beamed cottages, where they tend to be discordant with the cozy, country style of the architecture.

Just like glamorous patterns, bold patterns are ideal in "public" rooms. In hallways, living rooms, and dining rooms, they may take the form of upholstery or window treatments, wall or floor coverings, lampshades, or accessories such as cushions or china. These are the show-offs of the pattern world: they like an audience, and make great talking points for visitors.

In the kitchen, bold patterns are not quite so easy to use. They may still, however, work well as wall coverings or backsplashes (tiles, either large or mosaic tesserae, are ideal to create an eye-catching grid or striped design), as cupboard doors, either manufactured or painted in contrasting vivid colors, or dramatic accessories placed for display on open shelving.

Bedrooms and bathrooms, being private, intimate spaces, are rarely filled with bold pattern. Many people feel that bedrooms, in particular, should be made to feel calm and restful by restricting pattern to small scales and soft colors.

OPPOSITE Painting cupboard doors in varying shades of the same color is an inexpensive way to create dramatic interest in an otherwise simple kitchen. The vibrant, all-over print on the chair reiterates the bold red and adds quirky interest.

BELOW This stylized floral printed fabric, by Austrian architect and designer Josef Frank for Svenskt Tenn, has been carefully stretched over a wooden frame to create a colorful backdrop for mid-20th-century Scandinavian furnishings.

ABOVE **Dense blocks of strong color, stylized designs, and all-over patterns are characteristic of this look. Here, plain white, modern furnishings create the backdrop for colorful cushions and a tablecloth by renowned Finnish design firm Marimekko and black-and-white dishes by Missoni Home. It is essentially a simple scheme, but very effective.**

Nevertheless, all decorating is a matter of individual taste, and just because a convention exists does not mean that you have to abide by it. Breaking the rules often results in the most stunning results, especially from someone with a good eye, and large patterns can look incredible when used for bedroom walls, linens or flooring. And in the bathroom, bold patterning is marvelous on towels and bath mats, shower curtains and blinds, and could even be incorporated in tilework on floor or walls.

A word of warning might be timely at this point. Bold patterns can become outdated more quickly than others, or may become tiresome to live with after a while, however exciting at first. If the cost or aggravation of frequent redecorating is an issue, it would be wise to restrict bold patterns to areas that can be overhauled easily. Avoid using them for things that are built-in, glued down, or otherwise permanently fixed, unless they can be easily altered by some measure such as stripping or over-painting. Similarly, unless you are absolutely certain that you will be happy with them for a decent length of time, it might be better not to purchase expensive upholstery or curtains in bold designs, but instead restrict yourself to characterful cushions, vases, and lampshades—smaller items that can be changed easily and without enormous outlay.

THIS PAGE **This tiny London apartment has massive presence, thanks in large part to the dramatic pattern painted on the floor. Inspired by abstract, organic mid-century textile motifs by Jacqueline Groag and Josef Frank, it was painted by the owner himself.**

LEFT AND ABOVE A pink, red, and white pillow cover with a bold pattern of triangles coordinates perfectly with the pink geometric pattern of the wallpaper in this informal dining area. The colors are a lovely complement to the golden tones of the wooden dining table and chairs. The cushion is from Ikea, and the wallpaper by Jocelyn Warner, who is known for her striking, simple designs that have reinterpreted contemporary wall coverings. This image is called "Step," and was created by scanning folded paper into a computer. The resulting design has a three-dimensional feel, with designs that float up and down their columns and create an atmosphere that is both grand and elegant.

The best way to make sure you will love your bold patterns forever is to choose them with a combination of heart and head. There is no substitute for that gut-wrenching moment when you see a pattern that you fall head over heels in love with, but it is always best to give some logical consideration to the matter, too, before digging deep into your wallet. For example, does the scale suit the room where you intend to use it? In general, the bigger the room, the bigger the scale it can take, and very large patterns tend to look awkward in very small rooms. The exception is when you are happy for the room to feel busy or even claustrophobic.

THIS PAGE AND OPPOSITE
To use such a strong color as this pomegranate red in a bedroom is unusual, but here it clearly works. The painted walls are a dramatic backdrop for fabric designs by Ann Louise Roswald—stylized flowers and leaves in flat blocks of color, made up into cushion covers and a stunning patchwork quilt, with a dress hung on the wall like a work of art.

Then there is the question of color. Some people have an instinct for choosing and combining colors, while others find it tricky. If you are in the latter camp, then bold patterns, with their predisposition for strong colorways, should be treated with care. Start by choosing a "family" of no more than two or three complementary colors, and steer clear of any bold patterns that use anything other than those exact colors. A color wheel can be a great help. A circle divided into segments showing the primary (red, blue, yellow), secondary (purple, green, orange), and sometimes tertiary and other colors—somewhat like a rainbow that has been curved so that the ends join together—it is a device used by artists and decorators alike. Colors that are adjacent to or opposite each other on the color wheel will coordinate, albeit sometimes unexpectedly, such as fuchsia with crimson or blue with orange. More straightforwardly, darker and lighter shades of the same color always work well together. For further inspiration, observe naturally occurring color combinations, where colors can be surprisingly vivid and discordant, yet still look wonderful in conjunction with one another.

Having considered color and scale, it is worth obtaining large samples of patterned fabric or wallpaper and draping or hanging them in place to gain a really good idea of their effect. You may also wish to create a mood board, which many decorators use to make sure that all the ingredients of a scheme

ABOVE AND OPPOSITE **A great example of a bold pattern in a soft colorway, the silver-and-aqua-striped wallpaper is a highly contemporary flock by Osborne & Little. The cushions on the bed have been carefully chosen to reflect the aqua tone, and are in various patterns, ranging from Art Deco-inspired to more soft and romantic.**

relate well to each other and create the desired effect. A large sheet of cardboard is ideal as a background, on which you can paint background colors and stick swatches of pattern, along with sketches or images cut from magazines of furniture and accessories. If possible, it is best to keep the sizes of all the elements in proportion to the size at which they will eventually be used. By adding and removing different components, you should eventually reach an attractive and effective combination. Another potential concern is that one boldly patterned room does not conflict with another: it is best, when planning, to bear in mind the decoration of adjacent rooms so that there is some sort of continuity of color and scale between them.

The most straightforward way in which to use bold pattern is to choose just one pattern and make it the focal point of an otherwise understated room. You might, for example, keep walls and floors pale and plain, and simply add a brightly patterned armchair, or a bold curtain fabric. Alternatively, you could cover one wall with a distinctive paper, put down a rug with a dramatic design, or simply pop some vivid cushions onto a simple sofa. Restricting bold pattern to limited areas in this way helps to make sure it does not become overwhelming. For a more intense effect, you could install flooring or paint walls in a brighter or deeper (but still plain) color, ensuring that it coordinates well with one of the colors used in your pattern.

RIGHT The simple patterns of these Melin Tregwynt pillows and coordinating throw resist categorization, but their intense colors here, from turquoise through to navy, puts them in the bold-and-brave camp—albeit at the subtle end of the spectrum.

OPPOSITE A blue-painted wall makes this look appear more intense. Using a range of shades of one color is a straightforward way to apply pattern in the home to good effect.

When combining two or more bold patterns, the secret is to coordinate colors carefully, to ensure that their scales vary slightly but not too much, and to look for similarities in the patterns themselves, in terms of outline, form, density, and overall style. If they are too disparate, the scheme will fall apart. As with many decorating endeavors, the golden rule is that, if in doubt, you should take it out— Mies van der Rohe's maxim that less is more holds very true when applied (as he surely did not mean it to be) to the use of pattern.

Finding bold patterns to use in the home is not difficult. As pattern becomes increasingly fashionable, suitable fabrics, wallpapers, furnishings, and accessories are more and more readily available, both from chain-store and mall retailers and the more upscale design companies. A tour of the design shows, held once or twice yearly and most of them open to the general public, will offer an inspiring insight into the cutting-edge designs that are coming up, often from young, not-yet-established designers with innovative ideas. Sometimes they will sell straight from their stand; or you may have to note their details and contact them later. For something truly personal, you could commission a specialist company to produce a short run of a limited-edition or custom-made pattern, or even take an adult education class in screen- or block-printing and design and make your own lengths of fabric or paper.

The secondhand market has much potential, too, and it is possible to find superb examples of genuine retro fabrics at auction or through specialized dealers. Pieces by well-known designers are highly prized—and priced accordingly, but for next to nothing you can pick up all sorts of boldly patterned fabrics and accessories at estate clearances, garage sales, and yard sales. Many of them will be hideous: the trick is to choose the best and use them judiciously. Plates, vases, and glassware can make fantastic displays, while clean and not-too-worn-out clothing— perhaps silk scarves or men's shirts—could be transformed into cushion covers or lampshades. Smaller pieces of fabric could be framed just like a work of art (as can fragments of old wallpaper), while if they coordinate in color they could be made up into a patchwork and turned into gorgeous cushions, curtains, or quilts.

ABOVE AND OPPOSITE **Unless you decide to opt for the permanence of tilework, it can be hard to incorporate pattern in a bathroom. This is the ideal solution—towels in a range of strong colors and confident stripes and zigzags (instantly recognizable as by Italian label Missoni), which create excitement in an otherwise understated room that has been furnished with lovely, oversized old sanitaryware.**

SUCCESS WITH BOLD PATTERN

Dense, all-over, large-scale patterns in blocks of vibrant color are typical of this look, though you may prefer to choose paler or softer colors, or smaller-scale patterns in bright shades.

Bold patterns look particularly good in larger properties, especially high-ceilinged, rectilinear modern homes, or period properties that have a grand feel. However, they can also be used to dramatic effect in retro-style homes and in more modest spaces.

If you are at all unsure of how best to incorporate bold patterns into your home, start by introducing them in small doses, in ways that can easily be changed, such as pillows, towels, duvet covers, or lampshades. Limiting the colors and the types of pattern you employ will also make them easier to use. When you feel truly confident, you can add them more extensively and in more permanent ways.

They are really well suited to public rooms, such as hallways, living rooms, and dining areas, where they can be appreciated by you and your visitors alike.

A plain and understated background will help to ensure that bold patterns not only stand out, but also prevent them from becoming overwhelming. On the other hand, painting walls in a coordinating, vivid color, or choosing plain-but-bright upholstery as a backdrop, will give the look dramatic intensity.

Scale is an important consideration here, and most people like to use large-scale, highly colored patterns only in their biggest rooms, or else to restrict them to small doses (such as a wall print or cushion cover), where they will not be overpowering.

natural inspirations

From the most primitive of times, mankind has decorated the objects around him—his walls, drinking vessels, food containers—with patterns inspired by what he could see: the natural world.

A bird's plumage, a branch of blossoms, a snail shell, a honeycomb, the ripples created by dropping a pebble into a pond, fish scales, the grain of wood—all are examples of wonderful natural patterns that need no enhancement. We are surrounded by pattern and it is no wonder that patterns derived from nature are at the heart of our urge to decorate our homes.

Trees, foliage, and flowers, in all forms from extremely representational to highly stylized, are by far the most commonly occurring of all patterns, and have been so for centuries, especially in the western world. Appearing time and time again, from ancient Egypt to classical Rome, Renaissance Europe to modern times, the most popular motifs for pattern have always been the lotus, palmette, acanthus, "bent-leaf" or paisley, and pomegranate. The "tree of life" has been another enduring pattern

ABOVE Though oversized and designed with stylized flat blocks of color, the delicate eucalyptus branches that climb up this wallpaper have a naturalistic quality that is highly appealing, while its subtle color makes it very easy to live with.

OPPOSITE This wallpaper by Jocelyn Warner, simply called "Leaf," makes a lovely backdrop for a hand-thrown pot and a soft-toned oil painting, displayed on a white mantelpiece.

BELOW AND OPPOSITE This doodle-like pattern was made using ink drawings based on photography taken at London's Kew Gardens. They were manipulated in the computer and recolored. The pattern is actually strangely calming, particularly in combination with solid, plain, and geometric furniture.

since ancient times, while 'mille-feuilles' patterns of dense, all-over foliage and flowers have been used on items from 18th century Ottoman embroidery to 20th-century Scandinavia. From time to time, Europe has developed a craze for oriental designs, and chinoiserie-style patterns—from hand-painted walls with scenes of Eastern landscapes, trees, flowers, and birds, to Willow Pattern china, with its typical composition of willow tree, bridge, tea house, birds, and fenced garden—have now become very familiar. Today, natural patterns are derived from flora and fauna, just as they have always been, though the emphasis may be more on, say, petals, seed heads, or ferns rather than more traditional imagery.

Although natural inspirations could be said to apply to all types of pattern, what we mean in this chapter is a specific, modern type of natural pattern, with a look that is delicate and detailed, often romantic and ethereal, even other-worldly. What these patterns have in common is a very open, fresh feel. Backgrounds are nearly always pale, and the proportion of pattern to field is low—there may be a much greater area of plain background than there is of pattern itself. Colors are, if not monochromatic, generally quite limited, and are usually quite soft and subtle.

The most cutting-edge interpretation of this look employs innovative modern techniques, such as computer-enhanced imagery, digital printing, and laser-cutting,

to produce patterns that are pretty and appealing, but which also have a pleasingly contemporary aesthetic. They may use sinuous lines or solid sections of color, they often have a flattened, graphic quality and use surprising colors or play games with scale. This is a young look, very accessible and not necessarily at all expensive, and can often be applied in intriguing and unusual ways throughout the home.

A more traditional approach, on the other hand, involves time-honored craft techniques, such as hand-painting, needlepoint, or block-printing, and attempts to imitate nature in a fairly realistic way, with more accurate color renditions, three-dimensional shading, perspective, and a conventional use of scale. The feel is more illustrative, sketchy, or painterly than that of the more modern approach, and the look more mature, sometimes more expensive, though still just as delightful to use.

Either style of nature-inspired pattern is very easy to live with. It feels reassuringly familiar, and even in its most modern form is not in the slightest bit scary or difficult. These are forms that curve, twist, and twine across our rooms, embracing and comforting us, fostering an atmosphere of pleasure and relaxation. They never create discord or tension, but instead bring a sense of peace and tranquility. After all, who could feel stressed when looking at a reproduction of an attractive landscape or a beautiful flower? It may not be the same as going for a walk in the country, but bringing natural pattern into our

ABOVE Kaffe Fassett is famous for his innovative and intricate needle-points, worked in jewellike colors. This apple pattern is complemented by cushions with geometric designs, and a sofa upholstered with a bold, stylized fabric.

OPPOSITE This mural, featuring naturalistic palm trees, covers an entire wall and is a modern interpretation of classic 18th-century panoramic scenes.

homes is one way of importing the essence
of nature into our everyday lives. And not only
that, but their open style and gentle colors
mean that they are restful to look at, unlike
other types of pattern that employ dense
designs and vibrant colors for an entirely
different effect.

Nature-inspired patterns, whether
modern or traditional, really do suit any type
of property. The smallest city-center
apartment or the largest country mansion
could incorporate such patterns, and they

can complement ornate period features or be a foil to pared-down modern homes. They work with practically all styles of furniture, from antiques to retro to modern—though perhaps less so with really minimal pieces, especially if they are very hard-edged, machine-produced, and in man-made materials. In very broad terms, these patterns are best complemented by neutral, pale colors and simple, timeless furnishings—waxed, limed, or whitewashed wooden floors, painted walls, pared-down furniture, and unfussy fabrics. But whether your look is young and funky, industrial chic, seriously sophisticated or cozy country, there is probably room for natural pattern in your home, in some form or another.

LEFT French design company Atelier LZC produces intricate, fresh natural patterns. Here, one has been used as a tall, thin wall panel, its colors complemented by those of the upholstery and scatter cushions.

FAR LEFT A row of delicate floral screen-prints is the principal source of pattern in this living room.

RIGHT The graphic yet pretty quality of these pillow covers is typical of the nature-inspired style.

ABOVE RIGHT Atelier LZC also designs flat steel cut-outs, in the shapes of birds, butterflies, and flowers, which can be hung decoratively. They look particularly effective, as does the framed screen print, against a plain background.

The obvious place in which to use natural patterns is on the wall, where they are reminiscent of a window onto the outside world. Panoramic scenes that completely cover edge to edge and floor to ceiling make a stunning focal point for a room. Such scenes were enormously popular, especially for bedrooms, in the mid-18th century, when hand-painted wallpapers were imported in large quantities from China to England. Each roll was painted with slender trees, flowers, and birds and, when hung, would match up to form a complete whole. They were an expensive fashion, used only in the best houses, though eventually the look filtered down to the slightly less well-off, via English manufacturers who began to produce hand-painted and printed imitations. You can still, for a price, find companies or individuals to paint or print such panoramas for you, or, if you were artistically inclined, it would be an ambitious project to attempt yourself, armed with images that inspire you, suitable paints and a selection of brushes.

The 21st-century equivalent of these panoramic scenes are photographic prints, which can now be bought relatively cheaply. Usually of flowers or seed heads blown up to an enormous size, and in hyper-real colors, they look impressive and can be used in groups or, if large enough, as a single piece of wall art. Alternatively, to create a look that is utterly personal, have your own landscape or still-life photograph recolored, enlarged to any size you like, and transferred onto canvas.

You can create a slightly different effect using wallpapers that depict natural or organic images. These can be quite delicate or, for a more eye-catching look, employ huge repeats of an individual natural motif. Hang them together or, more subtly, as single decorative panels. Such wallpapers tend to be made by smaller companies or by

individuals, some of whom will allow you to choose your own colors or even work with you to produce a unique design. On a similar basis, it is possible to have ceramic wall tiles digitally printed with your own photographic image, or to buy them in a range of nature-inspired designs, which might include, say, a sunset, poppy field, or rippling water.

As a floor covering, natural images can be both attractive and striking. Floor areas are generally the largest easily visible surface in any room and, because a floor covering can be very dominant, most people choose fairly neutral designs. Dense, vividly colored patterns are often difficult to live with on the floor, but nature-inspired ones, with pale backgrounds and subtle imagery, can strike an ideal balance, neither brash nor bland.

Recently developed techniques have made it possible to print vinyl, ceramic, and even carpet tiles with digitally produced images, so you can almost literally walk on a lawn, a sandy beach, or even scattered rose petals. Choose from a selection of commercial designs, or work from your own photography to create a unique environment. For a warmer, softer feel, edge-to-edge carpets are, these days, available in a wider range of attractive patterns than they have been for years, including classic and fashionable florals, with either small or large motifs, softly colored or more vivid. Perhaps easiest of all, though, would be to add one or more rugs, which can be found in an endless array of shapes, sizes, and colors, to complement a nature-inspired scheme of almost any style. Particularly appealing are rugs with fairly large-scale, stylized images on a

ABOVE **This bright and airy dining room is decorated with a variety of fresh patterns. They include metal cutouts hanging on the wall, cushions and a printed tablecloth.**

OPPOSITE **In the simplest of kitchens, it is possible to use patterned accessories to create a pretty, and very livable, atmosphere. Here, the colors of the striped tablecloth perfectly complement those of the wall panels, china, vases, and towels.**

plain background—a style that is both
modern and gentle—or, for a more
conventional taste, flat-woven Aubusson rugs
with their intertwining flowers, leaves, and
scrolls in delicate color combinations.

   Nature-inspired patterns are particularly
appealing when used in the form of textiles:
upholstery, window treatments, bed linens,
table linens, throws, cushions, and the like.
In an otherwise neutral and minimal room,
for example, a blind printed with a fresh
floral in a subtle color can add just the right

amount of soft personality; the same goes for a carefully placed throw, a cushion, or even a towel. Even when used more extensively, these types of textiles are rarely overpowering—sofa covers, full-length curtains, tablecloths, and duvet covers can all look gorgeous in most environments. Natural patterns of the more modern type tend to be printed rather than woven, though they may incorporate other techniques such as embroidery, appliqué, or beading, and may use unusual dyes or intriguing textural effects—perhaps devoré, pleating, or lace—to create a uniquely contemporary look.

Many people find that natural patterns seem to emerge effortlessly around their homes, in a variety of forms, without much pre-planning. In the living room, for example, a delicate wallpaper could provide a calm backdrop for socializing or relaxing; the same goes for carpet, curtains, or upholstery, while throws and cushions add a

LEFT The natural shapes of leaves and lilies have been manipulated on a computer to create these very modern patterns. Though large, their simple colors and delicate outlines makes them relatively easy to use, especially in conjunction with plain furnishings.

OPPOSITE, LEFT The curtains are in a strong color, which matches that of the wallpaper pattern exactly.

THIS PICTURE AND OPPOSITE **This overscaled wallpaper pattern would, in a bolder color, be difficult to use, but in fact its blue/taupe pearlescence is absolutely charming, providing a backdrop that is interesting and contemporary, yet also surprisingly subtle.**

BELOW **The curving forms of this pendant light reiterate those of the wallpaper design.**

touch of prettiness, as do lampshades, framed prints, or other accessories. In the bedroom, a floral bedcover would set the tone for the entire room, as would a nature-inspired floor covering or window treatment. In a dining room or eating area, natural patterns on tablecloths, chair covers, napkins, or china make easy partners for food and entertaining, while in the bathroom they are a refreshing foil to hard, shiny surfaces.

Naturally inspired patterns are, in fact, enormously versatile, and are among the easiest to use of all. For such

ABOVE LEFT **No-color pattern can be highly effective. This plain white lampshade is made from laser-cut card, its delicate foliage shapes projecting a magical garden when illuminated.**

ABOVE RIGHT **This tiny bird, a detail from the mural that covers the bedroom walls, has been beautifully hand-painted.**

a scheme to appear really coherent and pleasing, however, it still helps to devote a certain amount of thought to it in advance.

The initial question is how dominant these patterns should be in the room. Depending on your style, they can be extremely subtle, hardly visible at all, or more noticeable, employed as an overall theme. Do you want to use them as well-placed details such as the occasional lampshade, a cushion here or there, a kitchen accessory such as a tea towel or an oven glove? Or more profusely, covering larger areas, perhaps as upholstery, curtains, or floor coverings? In terms of color, would you prefer pale, cool colors, or something a little stronger? Perhaps surprisingly, color schemes for these patterns do not have to be absolutely natural. In fact, naturalistic patterns can look stunning when designed in unusual colors or even with a soft pearlescent sheen. And would you prefer large- or small-scale patterning? The more grandiose the scale, the more contemporary the pattern will appear, particularly if repeated, but this will make it much more of a bold feature than if you restrict the size of the pattern.

For an unfussy, easy-to-live-with effect, it is best to use only one natural pattern in a relatively restricted way. It might be very simple in design, subtle in color, small in scale, or just used over a very limited area: this is pattern that is disciplined in usage, creating a modern look that manages to be at once soft and streamlined; clean-lined enough to satisfy a style-sophisticate, yet not so utterly minimal that it is hard and uninviting.

On the other hand, it is incredibly straightforward to combine these patterns. If you like the idea of layering and mixing nature-inspired patterns, follow the golden rules of coordinating colors exactly, and choosing scales that contrast a little, but not too much, and you cannot go too far wrong. Think of it as creating an appealing arrangement of flowers. You might start with blooms of one color, add a contrast, then put in just

LEFT The owner of this bedroom is a partner in French design company, Atelier LZC. Here, she has used wall panels, hanging metal cut-outs and cushions (by a colleague) to create a very personal space. The colors are highly unnatural and quite diverse, yet the delicacy of line and pale, open background means that the look is pretty and serene.

ABOVE The bedside tables are made using standard furniture from Habitat, with the addition of screen-printed panels created by the designer in her workshop.

a touch of a third shade that highlights the other two. As for size, you need to find flowers that are neither too different nor too similar. You would also consider form—spherical flowers contrasting with spearlike shapes and also spriggy blossoms. In terms of pattern, this might mean putting a block of color with an outline, plus something more sketchy. Another important point, in this case, is that the styles of pattern depiction should match. In other words, when you put realistically interpreted natural patterns alongside stylized ones, the effect is odd; put like with like, however, and everything will fall into place. It is possible to find plenty of nature-inspired patterns from individual designers and in the mall, in all forms, from fabrics and wallpapers to floor coverings and accessories. This is a look that stretches all the way from a high-end, high-budget style right through to the mass market. Many of the good department and chain stores have a wide selection of products that fit the bill, from cushion covers to china, bed linen to wallpapers. Alternatively, a tour of the design shows may result in finds that push back the barriers in terms of design and production techniques. The trick is to choose the best parts, the elements that suit you and your home the most, and to ignore the rest. For the very modern version of this look, keep an eye out for everyday objects that, though still functional, have become something really special through the use of this type of pattern: lampshades, for example, that have been laser-cut into intricate foliage shapes in order to cast intriguing patterns of light and shade, china that incorporates piercing and stitching, and wallpaper with embellishments such as embroidery and stickers. This may be one of the most ancient and familiar types of patterning but, depending on your approach to its use, it can be as avant-garde as you like.

OPPOSITE **This graceful twining floral wallpaper by Neisha Crossland is fashionable and feminine. Its black and ivory combination looks great with touches of pink elsewhere in the room.**

BELOW **The natural patterns in this funky bedroom—delicately outlined in variations of black, white, and gray—include peacock feathers, horses, birds, and a wallpaper of trees by Cole & Son.**

SUCCESS WITH NATURAL PATTERNS

For a fresh, modern look, choose nature-inspired patterns with a pale, open background and delicate designs in soft, muted colors, or perhaps with a pearlescent sheen. Techniques such as laser-cutting or computer-generated imagery give a cutting-edge aesthetic, or you could opt for a more traditional look, employing craft techniques such as hand-painting or needlepoint.

Nature-inspired patterns are really easy to live with, and suit any type of property, from period to modern. They look particularly good when teamed with neutral colors and timeless pieces of furniture that have unfussy shapes and pale colors.

Large-scale patterns have more presence, and are best used in subtle colors, particularly if repeated around the room. Smaller-scale patterns are easier to use, and can be in more vivid shades.

If you try to mix realistic depictions of natural pattern with stylized interpretations, you might find that the overall effect is rather odd. It is usually better to keep like with like.

Hand-painted or wallpapered murals that cover wall-to-wall and floor-to-ceiling are a dramatic interpretation of this look. Less extreme are large photographic or illustrated prints, which create a focal point in a room, or single panels of wallpaper with oversized motifs.

For the most interesting combination of nature-inspired patterns, use a variety of designs that each offer something different—blocks of color with illustrative outlines, rounded forms with long, thin shapes—but that reiterate colors and an overall style.

modern classics

Classics are the enduring designs of the pattern world. Good-looking and enormously versatile, they are unaffected by fads or fashion, and give a decorative scheme a mature and thoughtful edge.

These are the patterns that have recurred—in almost the same forms—for centuries. Scrolling patterns with arabesques and acanthus leaves, fleur de lys, trefoils and quatrefoils, borders and frames, knots and key patterns, garlands and medallions, laurel leaves and honeysuckle, Tudor roses, pomegranates, urns, and egg-and-dart: they originated in the Roman, medieval, or renaissance eras, but they can still look absolutely right in a 21st-century home. Most classic patterns are highly structured in design. Usually symmetrical, they might feature architectural, oriental, or stylized floral motifs, but they tend to appear organized rather than free-flowing, covering the background well but neither very densely nor very loosely. Their colors are similarly restrained, avoiding pastels and brights, but instead involving sophisticated, traditional shades such as claret, navy, chocolate, dark green, mustard yellow, ivory, and charcoal.

It is worth making a special mention here of toile de Jouy, which, as its name suggests, originated in Jouy-en-Josas, France, and is a printed cotton usually featuring pastoral or mythological scenes with figures, often in blue, black, red, purple, or sepia on white. The factory for printed cottons was

OPPOSITE **This delicately carved sofa has been covered in an antique Irish damask. The coordinating cushions were mostly found in a flea market in Florence, and the porcelain in the foreground is a design called "Flora," by Dutch firm Petrus Regout.**

ABOVE **The acanthus leaf pattern of this lampshade is in a subtle blue, which perfectly picks out the color of the Aubusson rug used as a wall hanging behind.**

LEFT Neutral walls, curtains, and furnishings enable classical patterns and accessories to stand out, and prevent them from looking too formal. This chaise longue has been draped with an old shawl to great effect. The cushion, with a fun marabou fringe, is in a fabric by Mariano Fortuny, a renowned Venetian artist/designer whose textiles were influenced by 15th-century Florence and 17th-century Venice, Persia, Asia, Egypt, and Greece. First produced in the early 20th century, his work soon became renowned for its beauty and versatility, and is still available today.

ABOVE This room has a classical feel, but pale walls and carpet, and the witty addition of a touch of animal print, bring a deft sense of individuality.

THIS PAGE AND OPPOSITE, LEFT
A classical flocked wallpaper suits
this grand living room perfectly,
and its neutral color is repeated by
the satin damask upholstery of the
sofa. With this backdrop, the room
could easily have developed a
grave, heritage-home atmosphere,
but because the owner has added
kitsch accessories and modern,
bright cushions, it actually has an
air of fun and frivolity.

OPPOSITE, RIGHT, ABOVE AND
BELOW The upholstery of the
sofa in the bay window of the
living room is in a design by
Florence Broadhurst. Flat, stylized
flowers and foliage reiterate those
of the gold wallpaper, also her
design, in the main hallway.

established in Jouy in 1760, and from 1770 it began producing the monochrome copperplate prints that soon became enormously fashionable in homes throughout Europe. Today, the term "toile de Jouy" is no longer a description of a place but of a style; the fabric could be produced anywhere in the world, though always has the distinctive one-color, finely engraved design, often with a narrative element.

Like toile, most classic patterns tend to be associated with traditional production methods—so, for example, wallpaper might be block-printed, flocked, moiré (with a wavy, watermarked appearance), or embossed, while fabric is more often woven than printed, using time-honored techniques such as damask, tapestry, or brocade, or employing luscious fabrics such as silk, satin, and velvet. Embellishments could include

tassels, fringes, tie-backs, ruffles, and buttoning, while elsewhere hand-knotted rugs, tapestry wall hangings, and hand-decorated ceramics might also figure.

What is great about using classical pattern is that it creates a very serene effect. It has character and presence, but doesn't show off about it. Neither bland nor bold, it works best in properties that have generous proportions and strong character of their own, whether modern or traditional. It is an ideal choice for a period home, where it will complement the architecture and overall style

superbly. Classic furnishings are its obvious allies. Choose dark, polished, or carved wood, buttonback upholstery, four-poster or tester beds, oil paintings, thick carpets, Venetian mirrors and so on—the look is one of elegance and understated luxury. On the other hand, for a more contemporary feel, period architecture and classic patterns can look amazing when combined with sleek, minimal, modern furnishings—the contrast adds a frisson of excitement to the overall scheme.

In the living room, classic patterns look wonderful used in the form of upholstery (chaises longues as well as sofas and armchairs) and curtain fabrics, as throws or cushions, carpets, and rugs, and, of course, wallpaper. They may sometimes create a rather formal atmosphere, which can be ideal for "public" living rooms (used for entertaining rather than relaxing and watching TV). The same goes for dining areas, where classically patterned table linen, china, wallcoverings, rugs, and accessories look both gracious and stylish. A tea service by one of the great china companies such as Wedgwood or Spode— complete with tea and coffee pots, charger, and cake stand—is ideal for either a dining room or kitchen, while in the bedroom these

OPPOSITE, LEFT The pretty china is a mixture of Dutch and French pieces, all in a delicate classical style.

OPPOSITE, RIGHT A delicate mobile is the center of attention in this otherwise subtle dining room.

ABOVE This room gives classical pattern an exotic twist. The Middle Eastern rug is typical of this look, but the chair upholstery is rather brighter than usual, and the needlepoint pillow covers add another jolt of color.

restrained patterns look marvelous when used for side chairs, bedcovers, and pillowcases, curtains or blinds, rugs, and lampshades. And in any room, of course, they are well accompanied by generous, carefully arranged displays of flowers.

All classic patterns have the ability to look completely timeless or absolutely fresh and contemporary. Color is often the key. The darker and muddier the shade of the pattern, the more likely it is that the overall look will be heavy and traditional; fresher, paler shades are always more modern—though brights are never a good idea. As a rule of thumb, neutral walls (preferably not bright white, which is not a truly historical color, but off-white, stone, or taupe) provide an excellent backdrop for classical patterns, allowing them to look their best without creating an oppressive atmosphere, which can be the case if walls are too dark.

Scale, as always with pattern, is another golden rule. Most classical patterns tend to be scaled to suit their usage—smaller patterns for a tea cup, larger ones for a wallcovering, and so on—so that the sense of discordancy, so characteristic of modern overscaling, is avoided. When designing an overall scheme, choose classic patterns with a scale that suits the size of your room. In a grand old house it is fine to use a huge pattern, but in a cottage or a more modern property, with lower ceilings and smaller rooms, something more modest is probably advisable.

To prevent classical patterns from giving an impression of imposing

OPPOSITE **Flat-woven Aubusson rugs were once made for the grandest French palaces and châteaux, reproducing typically classical motifs in soft colors. Here, the rug provides a gentle base for the room, with a damask-upholstered chair in the corner.**

ABOVE **What appears to be a painting is, in fact, a framed segment of antique hand-painted wallpaper.**

RIGHT Patterned china has been a kitchen staple for centuries, and can be as formal or informal as you wish. Whereas complete tea services were once de rigueur, it is now fashionable to mix and match—as long as you do it well. Here, the owner has kept things simple, and used just two patterns of blue and white, one of them a classic Willow pattern, for an appealing display.

BELOW Papering the inside of a cupboard door is a wonderful way to give yourself a treat when doing mundane tasks such as emptying the dishwasher or clearing up. This attractive paper is called "Hummingbird," by Cole & Son. Inside the cupboard is a selection of linens, glassware, and dishes, either family heirlooms or flea-market finds.

LEFT **A French-style carved and mirrored armoire has subtle surface patterning of its own, and reflects the eye-catching textiles used elsewhere in the room.**

formality, use them sparingly, against neutral walls, as above, and without going over the top on period detailing. Keep furniture that is both dark and heavy in form to a minimum, and remember that although swathes of swagged curtaining, miles of buttoning or piping, and wall after wall of busy wallpaper may all be typical of the way in which these patterns are often seen, they don't make for a stylish, livable home. Instead, opt for a more contemporary approach, with details such as simple gathered curtains or plain Roman blinds made from toile de Jouy, damask

cushions propped on a plain sofa, or a small needlepoint rug on pickled floorboards.

A restricted use of such patterns helps when it comes to budgeting, too. On the whole, superiority of material and manufacture matters more with this look than with others, making it a style that can be hard to create on a large scale if your finances are restricted. So, unless you are very good at searching secondhand shops and garage and yard sales for unexpected bargains, opt for using a small amount of good-quality pattern rather than reams of something cheap and

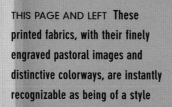

THIS PAGE AND LEFT **These printed fabrics, with their finely engraved pastoral images and distinctive colorways, are instantly recognizable as being of a style** known as toile de Jouy. Although pretty, toile can be overpowering, and here it has been toned down by the use of pale walls and bed linen as a calming backdrop.

cheerful. Employed as interesting details, against a background of coordinating colored plains, it will appear more fashionable, too. Of course, the ultimate choice, if your pockets are deep, is to buy from the renowned manufacturers of classical wallpaper, fabrics, and furnishings, whose designs are either reproductions of, or closely based on, genuine historical documents—or may even be patterns that the company has been producing for centuries without change. These are the firms whose reputation has stood the test of time and whose products are second to none. That said, of course, it is also worth exploring less expensive options, in the form of good-quality interpretations by modern companies, which may suit your overall look equally well.

LEFT **This dramatic library has been painted black, which perfectly offsets a luxurious Fortuny fabric cushion. On the shelves are leather-bound books, postcards from Venice, antique tassels, and a collection of other finds from around the world.**

OPPOSITE AND ABOVE **The same Fortuny fabric has been hung over the chimney breast, providing a backdrop for a framed collection of grasshoppers and locusts. The antique English double desk is piled with books and bits and pieces.**

SUCCESS WITH CLASSIC PATTERNS

Look for ordered, symmetrical patterns that are neither too dense nor too loosely spaced. Choose subtle colors and, in general, make sure the scale of the pattern is suitable for its application.

Traditional production processes and luxurious materials are typical, but can be expensive. Look for good-quality modern reproductions and try for antique bargains, but if in doubt choose the best quality you can afford and just use it sparingly.

Classic patterns are the natural choice for a period home. If you have large rooms with high ceilings, you can get away with pretty much anything, but if your property is low-ceilinged, perhaps a cottage or more modern in style, be careful about scale. Large-scaled classic patterns can be very dominant in a small space.

Don't go over the top in trying to recreate an authentic period interior. In most homes it is far better to opt for beautiful touches of classic pattern and steer clear of swagged and tailed curtaining, heavy carving, and overcrowded mantelpieces. Don't forget, less is more.

Period furniture is the ideal accompaniment to classic patterns, but avoid pieces that are very dark, or cumbersome in shape. Some Victorian (or Victorian-style) furniture, in particular, can be bulky, clumsy and not particularly attractive. Instead, delicate, Georgian or Louis-style pieces are better.

Walls painted or papered in a soft, neutral shade are a lovely backdrop to classical patterns, giving the look a fresh, modern feel. The same goes for simple curtains, upholstery, and other furnishings.

directory

ABC Carpet & Home
888 Broadway
New York, NY 10003
(212) 473-3000
www.ABC.com
An eclectic collection of linens, rugs, wall coverings, and decorative accessories for the home.

Anthropologie
1700 Sansom Street, 6th Floor
Philadelphia, PA 19103
(800) 309-2500
www.anthropologie.com
Vintage-inspired home accessories, hardware, bedding, and drapes.

Bedside Manor
715 Providence Road
Charlotte, NC 28207
(704) 334-5343
High-end linens and accessories for the bedroom.

Bella Linea Nashville
6031 Highway 100
Westgate Shopping Center
Nashville, TN 37205
(615) 352-4041
www.tpawebdesign.com/bellalinea
Exquisite linens, comforters, and bath accessories.

The Bombay Company, Inc.
P.O. Box 161009
Fort Worth, TX 76161
(800) 829-7789
www.bombaycompany.com.
Reproductions of classic, often British colonial-style home furnishings and accents, including wall decor and bedding.

Bremermann Designs
3943 Magazine Street
New Orleans, LA 70015
(504) 891-7763
www.neworleansantiquesdealers.com
Antique French linens and luxurious home accessories.

Calico Corners
www.calico corners.com.
Over 100 retail outlets discount a wide range of fabrics, trims, and select seconds. Affordable custom work also available.

Calvin Klein Home at Calvin Klein
654 Madison Avenue
New York, NY 10022
(212) 292-9000
Timeless linens, blankets, and throws.

Clarence House Fabrics, Ltd.
211 East Fifty-eighth Street
New York, NY 10022
(212) 752-2890
Natural fiber fabrics with prints based on 15th- to 20th-century documents. Also hand-woven textiles and fine wallpapers.

C.M Offray & Sons, Inc.
Route 24
P.O. Box 601
Chester, NJ 07930
(908) 879-4700
A wide selection of fabric, notions, and trims.

Crate & Barrel
650 Madison Avenue
New York, NY 10022
(212) 308-0011
www.crateandbarrel.com
A vast selection of rugs, curtains, home accessories, and more.

Discount Designer
1368 Barrowdale Road
Jenkintown, PA 19046
(215) 884-4923
www.discountdesigner.com
Online discount retailer of top wallpaper and fabric brands, including French Country, Pierre Dieux, Osbourne & Little, Souleiado, Oriental Wallpaper, and many more.

Dwell Home Furnishings
For mail only:
417 Canal Street
8th Floor
New York, NY 10013
www.dwellshop.com
Stylish modern textiles for the home; product lines include dwell, a contemporary adult bedding line, dwelltable, a mix and match table linens collection, and dwellbaby.

Eades Wallpaper and Fabric
307 North Union Street
Olean, NY 14760
Call (877) 229-9427
www.eadeswallpaper.com
Discount designer wallcoverings and fabric from Scalamandré, Thibaut, and Seabrook Wallcovering, and many more.

Garnet Hill
P.O. Box 262, Main Street
Franconia, NH 03580
(800) 870-3513
www.garnethill.com
An online retailer of duvets and pillows and linens all made from natural fibers.

Gracious Home
1220 Third Avenue
New York, NY 10021
(212) 517-6300
www.gracioushome.com
Bedding, linens, and other software.

Highbrow Inc.
2110 8th Avenue South
Nashville, TN 37204
(888) 329-0219
www.highbrowfurniture.com
Dealer of vintage modern furniture, textiles, and accessories.

Hinson & Co.
979 Third Avenue
New York, NY 10022
(212) 688-5538
Fabrics, coordinating wallpaper, and decorative accessories with an emphasis on clean, timeless design.

Jonathan Adler
1097 Madison Avenue
New York, NY 10028
(212) 772-2410
www.jonathanadler.com
Retro-inspired designs for pots, pillows, bed linen, and other home furnishings.

IKEA
1800 East McConnor Parkway
Schaumburg, IL 60173
(800) 434-4532
www.ikea.com
Inexpensive, functional home products for every room of the house.

Laura Ashley, Inc.
6 St. James Avenue
Boston, MA 02116
(800) 367-2000
www.laura-ashleyusa.com
English-garden-style floral, striped, checked, and solid cotton fabrics in a wide range of colors for every room in the house. Coordinated pillows, bedding, wallpaper, and trims.

Missoni Home at Missoni
1009 Madison Avenue
New York, NY 10021
(212) 517-9339
This boutique carries modern fabric designs, wall coverings, and soft furnishings.

Modhaus
Boston, MA
(617) 822-9183
www.modhaus.com
Online gallery of furnishings and decorative objects from the 1950s to 1970s, including Scandinavian designs and handcrafts. Must call ahead to visit the warehouse.

Modlivin
5327 East Colfax Avenue
Denver, CO 80220
(720) 941-9292
www.modlivin.com
Mid-century and modern furniture store with an online shop dedicated to new reissues and mid-century classics, including textiles and decorative accents.

On Board Fabrics
Route 27
P.O. Box 14
Edgecomb, ME 04556
(207) 882-7536
www.onboardfabrics.com
Fabrics range from plain cottons to Italian tapestry and woven plaids.

Oppenheim's
P.O. Box 29
120 East Main Street
North Manchester, IN 46962
(800) 461-6728
Mail-order retailer of country prints, mill remants, chambray, and more. For swatches on request, send a stamped self-addressed envelope.

Osborne & Little Inc.
979 Third Avenue, Suite 520
New York NY 10022
(212) 751-3333
www.osborneandlittle.com
A leading name in contemporary wallpaper and fabric design.

Peter Fasano, Ltd.
964 South Main Street
Great Barrington, MA 01230
(413) 528-6872
Carries antique and contemporary textiles.

Pierre Deux
879 Madison Avenue
New York, NY 10021
(212) 570-9343
www.pierredeux.com
*Fine French country
wallpaper, fabric,
upholstery, and antiques.*

Pierre Frey, Inc.
12 East Thirty-third
Street
New York, NY 10019
(212) 213-3099
*Fabrics and wall
coverings, including
printed cottons based on
an archive of 18th- and
19th-century French fabrics.*

Pottery Barn
600 Broadway
New York, NY 10012
(800) 922-5507
www.potterybarn.com
*Furnishing and decorative
accessories for the
contemporary home.*

**Ralph Lauren Home
Collection**
1185 Sixth Avenue
New York, NY 10036
(888) 475-7674
www.polo.com
*All-American accessories
for bed and bath from the
celebrated fashion designer.*

Repot Depot Fabrics
For mailing purposes
only:
116 Pleasant Street
Easthampton, MA 01027
(877) 738-7632
www.repotdepot.com
*Vintage reproduction and
retro-themed fabrics,
buttons, ribbons, and gifts.*

Restoration Hardware
935 Broadway
New York, NY 10011
(212) 260-9479
www.restorationhardware
.com
*Classic hardware and
software for the home,
from window and floor
treatments to bath
towels and bedding.*

Retromodern.com, Inc.
805 Peachtree Street, NE
Atlanta, GA 30308

(404) 724 0093
www.retromodern.com
*Online retailer of reissues
and current productions of
mid-century modern textiles,
rugs, pillows, and more.*

Rosebrand Textiles
75 Ninth Avenue
New York, NY 10011
(800) 223-1624
www.rosebrand.com
*Muslin, canvas, scrim,
ticking, and more.*

Salsa Fabrics
3100 Holly Avenue
Silver Spings, NV 89429
(800) 758-3819
www.salsafabrics.com
*Original fabrics in cotton,
silk, and wool imported
from Guatemala and
Indonesia.*

Smith + Noble
(800) 560-0027
www.smithandnoble.com
*Online store sells custom-
made (but affordable)
window treatments, pillows,
slipcovers, and duvet covers.*

Stitchin' Post
311 West Cascade
PO Box 280
Sisters, OR 97759
(541) 549-6061
www.stitchinpost.com
*Quilts, fabrics, and kits
by Kaffe Fassett and
other contemporary
designers; sponsors of
the annual Sisters
Outdoor Quilt Show.*

Takashimaya
693 Fifth Avenue
New York, NY 10012
(212) 350-0100
*This high-end Japanese
department store chain
features exclusive bed
linens, towels, and other
luxurious accessories for
the home.*

Textile Arts
P.O. Box 3151
Sag Harbor, NY 11963
www.txtlart.com
*Mail-order fabrics shop
specializing in Marimekko
fabric, linens, and wall
coverings.*

**Thibaut Wallpapers and
Fabrics**
480 Frelinghuysen Avenue
Newark, NJ 07114
(800) 223-0704
www.thibautdesign
*The wallpapers of this
elegant designer have
graced the walls of the
White House.*

Unica Home
7540 South Industrial
Road, Suite 501
Las Vegas, NV 89139-5965
(888) 89-UNICA
www.unicahome.com
*A wide range of modern
furnishing and home
accessories, both vintage
and reproductions by top
designers.*

Velocity Art and Design
2118 Second Avenue
Seattle, WA 98121
(866) 781-9494
www.velocityartanddesign.
com
*Textiles, rugs, pillows, and
pottery from mid-century
modern icons and emerging
classics, including the
Jonathan Adler Shop and
the Thomas Paul Shop.*

Wamsutta
Spring Industries Inc.
P.O. Box 70
Fort Mill, SC 29716
(800) 931-1488
www.wamsutta.com
*A wide range of
hardworking linens,
including flannels and
duvet covers.*

Waverly
(800) 423-5881
www.waverly.com
*An assortment of popular
window treatments, floor
coverings, decorative
fabric, and upholstery.*

West Elm
P.O. Box 29028
Brooklyn, NY 11202
(866) 428-6468
www.westelm.com
*Contemporary furniture
and home accessories with
a zen aesthetic.*

credits

PICTURE CREDITS

The publishers would like to thank all those who allowed us to photograph their homes for this book.

All photography by Claire Richardson

Key: **a**=above, **b**=below, **r**=right, **l**=left, **c**=center

Page **1 & 4c** Marianne Cotterill's house in London; **4r** Marcel Wanders and Peter Lute's hospitality & design creation Lute Suites in Ouderkerk aan de Amstel, on the outskirts of Amsterdam, The Netherlands www.lutesuites.com / tiles by Bizazza; **5** Available for photographic location at www.inspacelocations.com / "Painting By Numbers" canvas from Maisonette; **6–7** Fashion & textile designer Ann Louise Roswald's London home; **8** The London townhouse belonging to Louise Laycock of Bennison—watercolor and oil paintings by Jean Laycock / cushion by The Rug Company; **9** Interior design consultant Rachel van der Brug's home in Amsterdam / assorted fabrics sourced by Rachel van der Brug; **11** A family home in Blackheath, South London / "Cactus Paisley" wallpaper by Neisha Crosland; **12** "Malabar" wallpaper by Cole & Son; **14–15** Wallpaper by Marianne Cotterill; **16–18** Eifion & Amanda Griffiths of Melin Tregwynt's house in Wales / **16** "Mando" & "Madison" cushions and throws, lampshade, and spotted earthenware all by Melin Tregwynt; **17** "Madison", "Luna," & "Knot Garden" cushions and throws by Melin Tregwynt; **18** "Mando" & "Luna" designs by Melin Tregwynt; **19** A family home in Blackheath, South London / "Cactus Paisley" wallpaper by Neisha Crosland; **20–21** Marianne Cotterill's house in London; **22–23** The London townhouse belonging to Louise Laycock of Bennison—watercolor and oil paintings by Jean Laycock / cushion by The Rug Company, handmade patchwork tapestry by Louise Laycock, various fabrics by Bennison; **24–25br** Brandon Mably & Kaffe Fassett's family home in Hastings www.kaffefassett.com / handmade needle point tapestry and cushions by Brandon Mably and Kaffe Fassett; **25l & ar & 29** Marianne Cotterill's house in London / cushion from Maisonette; **26** various cushions by Designers Guild, rug by The Rug Company; **28** tapestry by The Rug Company; **30** Eifion & Amanda Griffiths of Melin Tregwynt's house in Wales / spotted earthenware by Melin Tregwynt; **32l & 33** Brandon Mably & Kaffe Fassett's family home in Hastings www.kaffefassett.com / handmade painted tiles by Kaffe Fassett; **34–35l** Marianne Cotterill's house in London; **35r–37 & 39** The London townhouse belonging to Louise Laycock of Bennison / framed fabrics by Bennison; **40–41** Marianne Cotterill's house in London; **42** The London townhouse belonging to Louise Laycock of Bennison—watercolor and oil paintings by Jean Laycock; **44** "Japanese Floral" wallpaper by Florence Broadhurst; **46–47** Fabric by Sanderson; **48–49** Available for photographic location at www.inspacelocations.com / "Chinoiserie" chinaware by Jasper Conran for Wedgewood, "Painting By Numbers" canvas from Maisonette; **50** Marcel Wanders and Peter Lute's hospitality & design creation Lute Suites in Ouderkerk aan de Amstel, on the outskirts of Amsterdam, The Netherlands www.lutesuites.com / tiles by Bizazza; **51–53** Available for photographic location at www.inspacelocations.com / vintage Pierre Cardin scarf turned cushion cover and "Painting By Numbers" canvas from Maisonette; **54** Marcel Wanders and Peter Lute's hospitality & design creation Lute Suites in Ouderkerk aan de Amstel, on the outskirts of Amsterdam, The Netherlands www.lutesuites.com; **55** Available for photographic location at www.inspacelocations.com / vintage scarves turned cushion covers from Maisonette; **56–61** Marianne Cotterill's house in London

/ various wallpapers by Florence Broadhurst; **62 & 63b** Marcel Wanders and Peter Lute's hospitality & design creation Lute Suites in Ouderkerk aan de Amstel, on the outskirts of Amsterdam, The Netherlands www.lutesuites.com / tiles by Bizazza; **63a–64a & br** Marianne Cotterill's house in London / various wallpapers by Florence Broadhurst; **64bl** Marcel Wanders and Peter Lute's hospitality & design creation Lute Suites in Ouderkerk aan de Amstel, on the outskirts of Amsterdam, The Netherlands www.lutesuites.com; **66** fabric by Svenskt Tenn; **68–69** Marcel Wanders and Peter Lute's hospitality & design creation Lute Suites in Ouderkerk aan de Amstel, on the outskirts of Amsterdam, The Netherlands www.lutesuites.com; **70** various cushions by Jonathan Adler at Century; **72–75** Graham Noakes of Osborne & Little's home in London / prints by Classic Prints, wallpaper and various fabrics by Osborne & Little; **76** Fashion & textile designer Ann Louise Roswald's London home / fabric by Ann Louise Roswald; **77** In the London apartment of author and journalist Bradley Quinn / fabric by Svenskt Tenn and cushions by The Cloth House; **78** black & white chinaware by Missoni, cushions and tablecloth by Marimekko; **79** In the London apartment of author and journalist Bradley Quinn; **80–81** Wallpaper designer Jocelyn Warner's house in London / wallpaper and fabric from Ikea; **82–83** Fashion & textile designer Ann Louise Roswald's London home / various fabrics by Ann Louise Roswald; **84–85** Graham Noakes of Osborne & Little's home in London / all fabrics and wallpaper by Osborne & Little; **86–87** Eifion & Amanda Griffiths of Melin Tregwynt's house in Wales / all fabrics by Melin Tregwynt; **88–89** A family home in Blackheath, South London / towels by Missoni; **90al & bl** Graham Noakes of Osborne & Little's home in London / print by Classic Prints, wallpaper by Osborne & Little; **90ar** Fashion & textile designer Ann Louise Roswald's London home / various fabrics by Ann Louise Roswald; **90br** A family home in Blackheath, South London, cushions by Missoni at Interdesign; **92–93** Hand-painted mural by Kaffe Fassett; **94–97** Wallpaper designer Jocelyn Warner's house in London / various wallpapers and lampshade by Jocelyn Warner; **98–99** Brandon Mably & Kaffe Fassett's family home in Hastings www.kaffefassett.com / mural by Brandon Mably & Kaffe Fassett, handmade patchwork fabrics (including curtains, cushions, and chaise longue) by Kaffe Fassett; **100–101** Barbara Zorn of Atelier LZC's flat in Paris / fabric, wallpaper and prints by Atelier LZC; **102–103** Brandon Mably & Kaffe Fassett's family home in Hastings www.kaffefassett.com / handmade needle point (including furniture covers) and hand-painted mural by Kaffe Fassett; **104–105** Barbara Zorn of Atelier LZC's flat in Paris / prints, chinaware, napkins and towel by Atelier LZC; **106–109** Wallpaper designer Jocelyn Warner's house in London / various wallpapers and bed cover by Jocelyn Warner; **110–111** A family home in Blackheath, South London / Hand-painted mural by D. Shoosmith www.dshoosmith.co.uk, lampshade by Lush Designs, bedspread and cushions by Linea Home at House of Fraser; **112–113** Barbara Zorn of Atelier LZC's flat in Paris / cushions, prints on wall and furniture, ceramics, and glassware by Atelier LZC; **114** A family home in Blackheath, South London / wallpaper by Neisha Crosland; **115** Marianne Cotterill's house in London / lampshade and fabrics by Florence Broadhurst, wallpaper by Cole & Son; **116al & bl** Barbara Zorn of Atelier LZC's flat in Paris / prints on wall and furniture, ceramics and glassware by Atelier LZC; **116br** Wallpaper designer Jocelyn Warner's house in London / wallpaper by Jocelyn Warner; **118–119** Wallpaper by Marianne Cotterill; **120–123** Interior design consultant Rachel van der Brug's home in Amsterdam / lampshade by Fortuny; **124–125** Marianne Cotterill's house in London; **125ar** fabric by Florence Broadhurst; **126** Interior design consultant Rachel van der Brug's home in Amsterdam; **127** Brandon Mably & Kaffe Fassett's family home in Hastings www.kaffefassett.com / needle point cushions and fabric for upholstery by Brandon Mably and Kaffe Fassett; **128–130l** Interior design consultant Rachel van der Brug's home in Amsterdam / wallpaper by Cole & Son; **131** A family home in Blackheath, South London; **134–136al** Interior design consultant Rachel van der Brug's home in Amsterdam / fabric by Fortuny; **136ar** A family home in Blackheath, South London; **136bl** wallpaper by Cole & Son; **139a** Marianne Cotterill's house in London; **139b** Fashion & textile designer Ann Louise Roswald's London home; **140** Marianne Cotterill's house in London; **144** The London townhouse belonging to Louise Laycock of Bennison.

BUSINESS CREDITS

ARCHITECTS & DESIGNERS

Ann Louise Roswald Ltd
The Toy Factory
11–13 Corsham Street
London
N1 6DP
UK
+44 (0)20 7250 1583
info@annlouiseroswald.com
www.annlouiseroswald.com
pages 6–7, 76, 82–83, 90ar, 139b

Atelier LZC
2 rue Marcellin Berthelot
93100 Montreuil
France
+33 1 42 87 81 34
+33 1 42 87 68 41
celine@atelierlzc.fr
www.atelierlzc.fr
pages 100–101, 104–105, 112–113, 116al–bl

Bennison Fabrics Ltd
16 Holbein Place
London
SW1W 8NL
UK
+44 (0)20 7730 6781
+44 (0)20 7823 4997
bennisonfabrics@btinternet.com
pages 8, 22–23, 35r–37, 39, 42, 144

Brandon Mably
www.brandonmably.com
pages 24–25br, 32l & 33, 98–99, 102–103, 127

Jocelyn Warner
3–4 Links Yard
Spellman Street
London
E1 5LX
UK
www.jocelynwarner.com
simon@jocelynwarner.com
pages 80–81, 94–97, 106–109, 116br

Kaffe Fassett
www.kaffefassett.com
pages 24–25br, 32l & 33, 92, 98–99, 102–103, 127

Lute Suites
Amsteldijk zuid 54–58
1184 VD Ouderkerk aan
de Amstel
The Netherlands
+ 31 (0)20 4722462
+ 31 (0)20 4722463
info@lutesuites.com
www.lutesuites.com
pages 4r, 50, 54, 62 & 63b, 64bl, 68–69

Maisonette
79 Chamberlayne Road
London
NW10 3ND
UK
www.maisonette.uk.com
+44 (0)20 8964 8444
+44 (0)20 8964 8464
pages 5, 48–49, 51–53, 55

Marcel Wanders Studio
Jacob Catskade 35
1052 BT Amsterdam
The Netherlands
+ 31 (0)20 422 1339
+ 31 (0)20 422 7519
www.marcelwanders.com
pages 4r, 50, 54, 62 & 63b, 64bl, 68–69

Marianne Cotterill (shop)
4a–5a Perrins Court
London
NW3 1QR
UK
+44 (0)20 7435 2151
pages 1, 4c, 14–15, 20–21, 25l & ar, 29, 35l, 40–41, 56–61, 63a–64a & br, 115, 118–119, 124–125, 139a, 140

Melin Tregwynt
Castlemorris
Haverfordwest
Pembrokeshire
SA62 5UX
UK
+44 (0)1348 891 644
+44 (0)1348 891 694
info@melintregwynt.co.uk
www.melintregwynt.co.uk
pages 16–18, 30, 86–87

Osborne & Little Ltd
Showroom
304 King's Road
London
SW3 5UH
UK
+44 (0)20 7352 1456
+44 (0)20 7351 7813
www.osborneandlittle.com
pages 72–75, 84–85, 90al & bl

index

Italics indicate captions.

acknowledgments

I would like to thank Anne-Marie Bulat and Alison Starling for giving me this wonderful opportunity to work on such an exciting project. Thank you to Pamela Daniels for her creative eye, design expertise, and beautiful layouts. I would like to thank Katherine Sorrell for researching and articulating this complex and varied subject so passionately and with such insight. I would also like to thank Miriam Hyslop for all her literary support and guidance. Many, many thanks go to all the people who welcomed us, with such generosity and hospitality, into their beautiful homes.

I would like to give special thanks to my pattern partner—the lovely and supremely talented Claire Richardson for her enthusiasm, charm, and exquisite photography. Thank you to Gabs and James for their invaluable assistance. Finally I would like to thank my husband Patrick for his support and for looking after Rosie and Sam while I was working on this project.

Sally Conran